The Coronaggadah

celebrating our coming forth
from quarantine into freedom

Dedicated to my Nanny, Freda Sack, who died before I was old enough to attend one of her legendary seders but who bequeathed to me her pot roast recipe, her Tiffany flatware, and the Sack family tradition of joyful irreverence.

And to my mom.

INTRODUCTION

When New York went into lockdown in March of 2020, one of the first things I had to do was cancel our Passover seder. Which made me sad. But I thought, "Well, I'll just have a dinner party this summer for all my usual seder guests." But summer stretched to fall, to winter, to 2021. Another spring without a seder, another year of isolation and frustration.

Finally, in October of 2021, it was considered safe for a group of up to ten people to gather outdoors. And so, I held an Un-Seder. All the trappings of a traditional seder, but instead of sharing the biblical story of Exodus from Egypt, we recounted the story of the pandemic. We gathered; we ate; we drank; and we celebrated our coming forth from quarantine into freedom.

The Coronaggadah was born.

You don't have to be observant, or even Jewish, to join the celebration. Covid disrupted the lives of everyone around the globe and the feeling of relief at having survived the worst of it is universal.

Maybe you're happy that the pandemic has gotten to the point where you can have a few friends over to enjoy some togetherness. Seeing the smiles on unmasked faces, sharing a laugh with a vaccinated colleague or even, dare I say, giving a hug to a pal you haven't seen in person for two years.

Maybe you're reading this in 2122 and you want to know what Covid was, how it affected people and how we ultimately came out the other side of the crisis.

Maybe you're bored with the traditional Haggadah and want to spice up the tale of the Exodus with some tales of the CovExodus.

Or maybe you just want an excuse to hang with friends and drink four glasses of wine.

Whatever your reason, this book is for you.

Behold this cup of wine! Let it be a symbol of our joy tonight as we celebrate the corning forth of our people from quarantine into freedom.

On this night, not long ago, we put down the remote, put on something other than sweatpants, and went outside to relish the glorious crowds, and noises, and smells of our beloved city, summoning all the peoples throughout the world to vaccinate, arise, and be free.

KIDDUSH

Since this isn't really a religious event, we won't say the traditional prayer over the wine. I offer instead the following toast to enduring friendship, with all due credit to Stephen Sondheim (and a shout out to Alix Friedman for the translation):

LECHAYENU	לחיינו
MIKAMONU	מי כמונו
EIN ALEINU	אין עלינו

HERE'S TO US, WHO'S LIKE US? DAMN FEW.

Drink the first cup of wine.

WASH THE HANDS רחץ

For generations, we have been told by the Haggadah to wash our hands. Now we know why. Seriously, people. Pandemic or not, please wash your hands.

PARSLEY כרפס

Parsley, lettuce or watercress, dipped in salt water, is distributed to all present, who say:

These greens are a symbol of the grocery workers, Instacart shoppers and restaurant delivery people who worked throughout the pandemic to ensure that the rest of us could stay home, safe and nourished. Let us say together:

TO-DAH RU-BAH תודה רבה

THANK YOU VERY MUCH.

MAROR מרור

We eat the maror, or bitter herbs, because the virus embittered the lives of our first responders, doctors, nurses, and all those who risked their lives daily to help others. And in memory of the many thousands of lives lost.

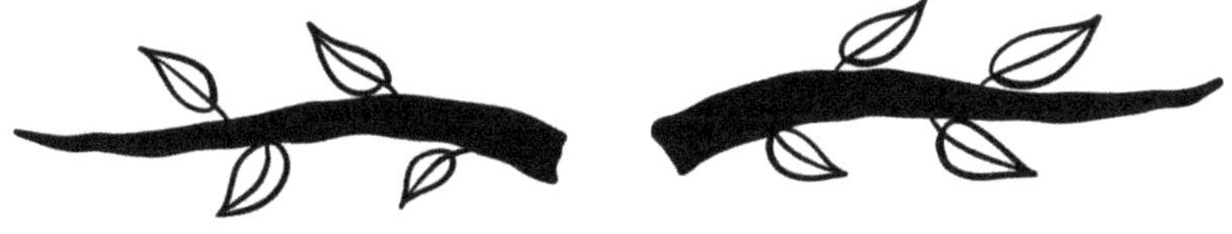

DIVIDE THE MATZAH

The leader breaks the middle matzah, leaving one half on the Seder dish and hiding the other half as the aficovid until the end of the meal. Before hiding the aficovid, she raises it and says:

There are three pieces of matzah on the plate, as the matzah represents three things. First, it is a symbol of the unleavened bread we ate throughout the lockdown, because stores had stocked up on it for the holidays anyway and all other carbs were sold out. Or,maybe we were lucky enough to find a bagel or two, so this is a reminder that even in a crisis, H&H delivers.

There is another meaning of the matzah. Before the virus, people ate in restaurants, coffee shops and Starbucks. No one thought of that as luxury, but now we know that even an unleavened piece of dough that tastes like cardboard is a beautiful thing if it's brought by a waiter in a fancy bread basket.

The middle piece is the aficovid, which is hidden somewhere in the house and represents that rare and elusive commodity that we hoarded in the early days of the pandemic: toilet paper.

THE FOUR QUESTIONS　　　מה נשתנה

The youngest child present asks the following questions:

מַה נִּשְׁתַּנָּה הַלַּיְלָה הַזֶּה מִכָּל הַלֵּילוֹת?

שֶׁבְּכָל הַלֵּילוֹת אָנוּ אוֹכְלִין חָמֵץ וּמַצָּה.
הַלַּיְלָה הַזֶּה כֻּלּוֹ מַצָּה:

שֶׁבְּכָל הַלֵּילוֹת אָנוּ אוֹכְלִין שְׁאָר יְרָקוֹת
הַלַּיְלָה הַזֶּה מָרוֹר:

שֶׁבְּכָל הַלֵּילוֹת אֵין אָנוּ מַטְבִּילִין אֲפִילוּ פַּעַם אֶחָת.
הַלַּיְלָה הַזֶּה שְׁתֵּי פְעָמִים:

שֶׁבְּכָל הַלֵּילוֹת אָנוּ אוֹכְלִין בֵּין יוֹשְׁבִין וּבֵין מְסֻבִּין.
הַלַּיְלָה הַזֶּה כֻּלָּנוּ מְסֻבִּין:

Why is this night different from all other nights of the year? On all other nights, we eat either leavened or unleavened bread; *why on this night do we eat only matzah, which is unleavened bread?* On all other nights, we eat vegetables and herbs of all kinds; *why on this night do we eat bitter herbs especially?* On all other nights, we never think of dipping herbs in water or in anything else; *why on this night do we dip the parsley in salt water and the bitter herbs in haroset?* On all other nights, everyone sits up straight at the table; *why on this night do we all recline at the table?*

THE NARRATIVE

The leader replies to the child:

I'm glad you asked the questions you did, for although they may sound just like the four questions from the traditional Haggadah, the answers from the Coronaggadah are quite different.

Why is this Seder different from all other Seders? While all other Seders celebrate freedom from slavery, tonight we celebrate the freedom to shop and dine out, attend a Broadway show, or cough in public without scattering strangers in all directions. But freedom from slavery is good, too.

Why do we eat only matzah tonight? I just told you that two pages ago. Are you stupid or were you too busy flipping ahead to see when the meal is served?

Why do we eat bitter herbs on this night? Tonight we commemorate the bitterness of quarantine and social isolation, the tragedy of lives lost, the sadness of unemployment and economic uncertainty, and we pray that we will never again be forced to endure such conditions.

Why do we dip the herbs twice tonight? We have already heard that we dip the parsley in salt water to honor the grocery workers and delivery people who worked throughout the crisis so that we may eat. We dip the maror, or bitter herbs, in the sweet haroset as a sign of hope, and to honor all those who gave us light and hope daily, from the doctors and nurses on the front lines to the performers and artists who shared their talents on Facebook and Instagram and reminded us that we're all in this together.

Why do we recline at the table? Tonight we remember day after day of social distancing when we could behave however we wanted because nobody was looking, so we ate dinner lying on the sofa binge watching Netflix.

Now let us recite the story of Covid as we find it in The New York Times and in the writings of the Internet.

Once we were locked down in our apartments, but science, truth, and common sense brought us forth and led us to freedom. If these things had not prevailed, we and our children and our children's children would still be cooped up, although how we would even have future generations with everyone practicing social distancing is a subject for another time. Therefore, even if we were all wise people, with long experience and PhDs in biology, it would still be our duty to tell and retell the story of the CovExodus from quarantine. In truth, the more we dwell upon the story of the CovExodus, the deeper will be our understanding of what freedom means, and the stronger our determination to win it for ourselves and for others.

The Rabbis and pundits used to tell and retell the story of Covid, in an attempt to be heard above the noise and misinformation. There is a legend of five Rabbis who became so interested in talking together about protecting Americans from the virus that they stayed up all night. As the story goes:

Once upon a time Rabbi Fauci, and Rabbi Cuomo* and Rabbi Tedros Adhanom Ghebreyesus of WHO, and Rabbi Birx and Rabbi Biden were feasting together in the village of District of Columbia and they talked about Covid for so long that before they knew it, it was morning and their students were calling to them, "It is already morning, it is time to convene the daily briefing."

**note: As of this printing, Rabbi Cuomo has resigned in disgrace for being an asshole, but in the summer of 2020 he showed great leadership at a time that it was sorely lacking from the White House. Thus his inclusion in this group.*

THE FOUR KINDS OF CHILDREN

Thus the story of the CovExodus will be told and re-told for generations to come. Parents will tell it to their children, who will tell it to their children, and so on. They will learn new words and phrases like "antigen test," "KN95," and "social distancing". The tale of America's recovery will always fill the children with wonder. But children are not all alike, as our Rabbis discovered many centuries ago. Some are curious, others are easily bored. Some are shy and some are belligerant.

In all, the Rabbis identified four kinds of children. Each one quite different from the rest, and each needs to be told the story of the CovExodus in a different way.

THE FIRST KIND OF CHILD IS THE WISE CHILD. She loves science; she is eager to learn everything about the virus and she asks, "What are the rules and conditions that doctors and scientists are saying must be in place for us to be safe?" First, she must be told all there is to know about social distancing, hand-washing, and mask-wearing. Then you must point out that, although we made it through a terrible time by following the guidelines, if we don't get to a hairdresser soon we're going to lose our minds.

THE SECOND KIND OF CHILD IS THE IRREVERENT CHILD. He is scornful. He thinks the whole thing is a hoax made up by Democrats and Commies and has always resented staying at home in the first place. He asks, "What does this virus mean to you?" He says "to you" as though he were an outsider who had nothing to do with it. This is as bad as equating public health protections with an assault on civil liberties. He should be scolded and told, "Try watching something other than Fox News, you ignorant moron. And maybe read a book."

THE THIRD KIND OF CHILD IS THE SIMPLE CHILD. She is naive and innocent, and she is very shy. She would like very much to know what Covid is, but just doesn't know how to ask about it. So she says, merely, "What is this all about?" She should be told, "The world was in the grip of a terrible pandemic, but Dr. Fauci, the scientists who developed the vaccines, and other wise people guided us through it and out of quarantine."

THE FOURTH KIND OF CHILD is the one who does not even realize that something unusual is going on. Therefore you must simply tell him, "This is because Dr. Fauci says it's finally okay for us to safely return to our lives."

HOW COVID-19 CAME TO AMERICA

The story begins very far away in a food market in Wuhan, China. While the source of the virus has yet to be 100% confirmed, most scientists believe that, like other coronaviruses, it originated in bats and somehow jumped to a single human, thus beginning a pattern of human-to-human transmission, eventually spreading throughout the globe. Within a month of it first appearing, The World Health Organization had declared it a global health emergency.

The virus, now named Covid-19, wreaked worldwide havoc, from a cruise ship quarantined in a harbor in Japan with hundreds of passengers testing positive, to early spikes in Italy and New York, to new variants evolving, to its eventual reach so far of 221 countries and territories with over 432 million confirmed cases and more than 5.9 million recorded deaths worldwide.*

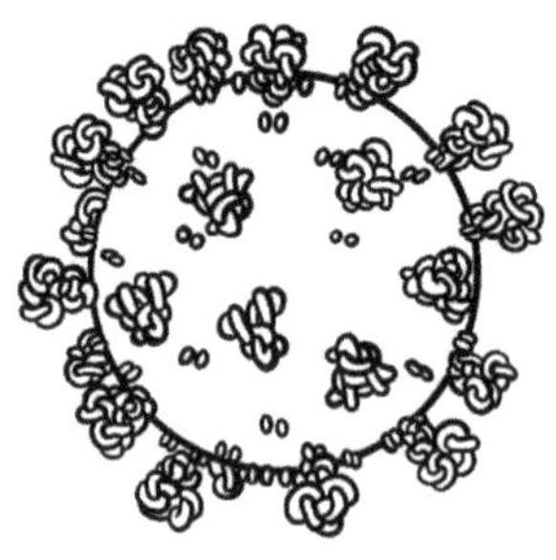

**Statistics current as of February 25, 2022 and are certainly higher by the time you read this. They also don't reflect the likely underreporting caused by insufficient testing, or the numbers that former Governor Cuomo fudged from nursing homes.*

THE SUFFERING OF NEW YORK

Although the first known Covid-19 patient in America was recorded in Washington State, New York quickly became the hardest hit area in the country. Hospitals were overwhelmed, protective equipment was in short supply, and many people were dying.

Soon, New York began to feel the effects of both the virus and the social distancing needed to slow the spread. Museums, restaurants, and retail stores closed. Broadway went dark. Classrooms transformed overnight into distance learning with teachers struggling to adapt and parents trying to combine working at home with caring for anxious and always-home kids.

HOW CUOMO CALMED NEW YORK

While the President's daily briefings were a symphony of self-congratulation and a medley of misinformation, Governor Cuomo presented the facts, explained the science and gave New Yorkers the leadership we needed in a crisis. We now know he was also hiding some crucial statistics, not to mention some inappropriate groping and touching, and he resigned in disgrace, but at the time he was a welcome and badly needed source of mostly accurate information.

Amidst all the suffering, there were signs of hope as New Yorkers followed the guidelines to protect themselves and each other, and, in response to Governor Cuomo's plea, people from around the country offered help. States with fewer cases delivered ventilators; thousands of health care professionals came to volunteer.

But even with all that was done to flatten the curve, the risk remained great and the country remained ill-prepared and way behind on testing because so much depends on great leadership which, alas, the country lacked.

TRUMP: THE MALIGNANT NARCISSIST

Like the ancient Pharaoh who ruled over Israeli slaves, Donald Trump represents every tyrant, every empathy-lacking, self-promoting, pussy-grabbing villain who has used the power of his position to enrich himself and his friends while undermining any attempt by his staff or Congress to preserve the tenets of democracy.

He cast blame, deflected responsibility, insulted reporters, applauded his TV ratings, and called the virus a hoax while people died and first responders and hospitals begged for ventilators and PPE.

Trump is a symbol of all those tyrants who ever acted as though they were gods, and whose will had to be obeyed without question, on penalty of unemployment or tweet.*

** For the record, the only words in this paragraph I changed from the original Haggadah were "Trump," "unemployment," and "tweet".*

And yet, in spite of President Trump's lack of leadership, Dr. Fauci went on talk show after talk show to correct the lies and misinformation; scientists worked tirelessly on vaccines and antibody tests; some governors coordinated to assure a gradual and safe return to normalcy; and slowly the country opened up again.

And that is why the CovExodus celebration means more than this current emancipation from quarantine. It means the millions of lives saved by Pasteur's work with bacteria, the emancipation from the polio epidemic won with the Salk vaccine, the resignation of Nixon after Woodward and Bernstein reported the Watergate scandal, the dismantling of the Berlin Wall. It means the inevitable triumph of truth, science, and human decency over adversity.

THE PLAGUE OF PRESS CONFERENCES

While President Trump's daily briefings were almost always cause for despair, some comments are likely to stand the test of time and remain symbols of his horrific response to the crisis. Even as we celebrate our newfound freedom, we remove a drop of wine from our glass for each comment which, by displaying his arrogance, incompetence, and narcissism represents preventable deaths.

We say together, and this is a direct quote from the original Haggadah as it needs no revision to be relevant today:

Each drop of wine we pour is hope and prayer
that people will cast out plagues that threaten
everyone everywhere they are found,
beginning in our own hearts.
The making of war,
the teaching of hate and violence,
despoliation of the earth,
perversion of justice and of government,
fomenting of vice and crime,
neglect of human needs,
oppression of nations and peoples,
corruption of culture,
subjugation of science, learning, and human discourse,
the erosion of freedoms.

WE POUR TEN DROPS FOR THE "ALTERNATIVE FACTS"

"We have it totally under control. It's one person coming in from China. And we have it under control. It's going to be just fine."

"There's a theory that, in April, when it gets warm - historically, that has been able to kill the virus."

"It's going to disappear. One day- it's like a miracle."

"If you go back six months or three months ago, nobody would have ever predicted."

"We are way ahead on testing. We are the best in the world on testing."

"I don't believe you need 40,000 or 30,000 ventilators."

"Chloroquine...may work, it may not work. I feel good about it. It's just a feeling. I'm a smart guy."

“The Wall Street Journal always ‘forgets’ to mention that the ratings for the White House Press Briefings are ‘through the roof’"'

“I see the disinfectant, where it knocks it out in a minute, one minute. And is there a way we can do something like that by injection inside or almost a cleaning?”

"No, I don't take responsibility at all."

DAYENU

The leader recites the verse and the company repeats the refrain, "Dayenu," which means "For that alone we should have been grateful."

HOW MANY SELFLESS DEEDS DID NEW YORKERS PERFORM FOR EACH OTHER!

Had they sheltered at home but not learned how to work remotely,

Dayenu!

Had they learned how to work remotely but not navigated their children's distance learning, anxiety, and cabin fever,

Dayenu!

Had they navigated their children's moods but not welcomed nurses and doctors who came from around the country to help,

Dayenu!

Had they welcomed nurses and doctors who came from around the country to help but not sewn masks out of old sheets,

Dayenu!

Had they sewn masks out of old sheets but not waited patiently six feet apart from each other in line at Trader Joe's,

Dayenu!

Had they waited patiently six feet apart from each other in line at Trader Joe's and not gone shopping for neighbors who were at high risk if they went out,

Dayenu!

Had they gone shopping for neighbors who were at risk if they went out and not applauded our healthcare workers every night at 7pm,

Dayenu!

Had they applauded our healthcare workers every night at 7pm and not posted video of Brian Stokes Mitchell singing "The Impossible Dream" out his window to first responders,

Dayenu!

How much more then, are we to be grateful to New Yorkers for the wonderful deeds they performed for us! For they sheltered at home and learned how to work remotely and posted and navigated their children's distance learning, anxiety and cabin fever and welcomed nurses and doctors who came from around the country to help and sewed masks out of old sheets and waited patiently six feet apart from each other in line at Trader Joe's and went shopping for neighbors who were at high risk if they went out and applauded our healthcare workers every night at 7pm and posted video of Brian Stokes Mitchell singing "The Impossible Dream" out his window to first responders!

LECHAYENU	לחיינו
MIKAMONU	מי כמונו
EIN ALEINU	אין עלינו

HERE'S TO US, WHO'S LIKE US? DAMN FEW.

Drink the second cup of wine.

WASH THE HANDS רחץ

For the second time tonight, we wash our hands. Those ancient Hebrews were on to something.

Praised be thou, O Gojo Industries, makers of Purell, and Proctor and Gamble, purveyors of toilet paper, cleansers and disinfectants (which we won't ingest).

BENEDICTION OVER MATZAH מוציא מצה

The leader distributes portions of the upper mazzah. Then all say together:

Praised be thou, O Trader Joe's and Seamless, Whole Foods and Instacart, and all those who kept us fed in times of peril.

BITTER HERBS מרור

The leader distributes a portion of bitter herbs, which is placed between two pieces of mazzah.

Praised be thou, O Amazon Prime and Netflix, who hast provided us with hours of entertainment to enable us to endure the bitterness of lockdown.

THE HILLEL SANDWICH 

The leader distributes a second portion of bitter herbs, which is placed with haroset on a piece of matzah, and says:

As the great Hillel used to do, and I mean the biblical sage, not the college group that rings in each Shabbat with a keg and a prayer, we add the bitter herb to the sweet haroset. This is a symbol of the sweetness that can come, even amid great bitterness, like the many acts of selflessness and kindness we have seen throughout this pandemic.

All eat the Hillel Sandwich.

THE MEAL IS SERVED

AFICOVID

Everyone searches for the hidden piece of matzah. Traditionally, the service can't continue until the leader negotiates its return with whoever finds it. But there's not much left but some fun stuff and two glasses of wine, so let's move things along.
Whoever finds it wins a free covid self-test.

The third cup of wine is filled, and the leader says:

We now fill our cups, for the third time, in thanksgiving for the festive meal which we have just eaten.

Let us say grace.

All say together:

Grace.

The leader raises the cup of wine and says:

As we drink the third cup of wine, let us all say together:

LECHAYENU	לחיינו
MIKAMONU	מי כמונו
EIN ALEINU	אין עלינו

HERE'S TO US, WHO'S LIKE US? DAMN FEW.

Drink the third cup of wine.

THE CUP OF FAUCI

This cup of wine is for Dr. Fauci. For, although we are celebrating our freedom, we know that this crisis is far from over and we depend on Dr. Fauci, the CDC, and all the other scientists and experts to guide us through the coming months and help us to all get vaccinated and do our best to prevent another spike of infections.

Let us sing together the song of Fauci (to the tune of "Eliyahu Hanavi"), and pray that he will continue to guide us and inform us.

Dr. Fauci, we know you're tired.
But Dr. Fauci, you're so admired
Trump didn't heed you,
but we still need you,
We're glad he's the one the country fired.

A RIDDLE OF NUMBERS

I'll tell you a number and you must say
The meaning it has for us today.
The number one I have in mind;
My meaning what wise child can find?

I know the meaning of number one
One stands for the day the pandemic's done

Who knows the meaning of number two?
If you know the answer, tell me true.

The two types of tests that were run
When our fight with the virus had just begun
One stands for the day the pandemic's done

Who knows the meaning of number three?
If you know the answer, tell it me.

Three stands for the three approved vaccines
That knock Covid to smithereens.
Two is the types of tests that were run
One stands for the day the pandemic's done

Who knows the meaning of number four?
If you answer that, I'll ask some more.

Four streaming services on our screens
When binge-watching became routine
Three stands for the three approved vaccines
Two is the types of tests that were run
One stands for the day the pandemic's done.

Who knows the meaning of number five?
What it means has kept our people alive.

Five stands for the types of financial assistance
That got us through pandemic existence
Four streaming services on our screens
Three stands for the three approved vaccines
Two is the types of tests that were run
One stands for the day the pandemic's done.

Who knows the meaning of number six?
A fact well-learned in the memory sticks.

Six stands for the feet of social distance
We keep at the CDC's insistence
Five stands for the financial assistance
Four streaming services on our screens
Three stands for the three approved vaccines
Two is the types of tests that were run
One stands for the day the pandemic's done.

Who knows the meaning of number seven?
In our city's compassion the meaning is given

Seven stands for the time that every night
We cheered for the front-liners in this blight
Six stands for the feet of social distance
Five stands for the financial assistance
Four streaming services on our screens
Three stands for the three approved vaccines
Two is the types of tests that were run
One stands for the day the pandemic's done.

Who knows the meaning of number eight?
Answer promptly: don't make us wait.

Eight stands for the eight days a week they'd fight
The nurses and doctors, those angels in white
Seven stands for the time we cheered each night
Six stands for the feet of social distance
Five stands for the financial assistance
Four streaming services on our screens
Three stands for the three approved vaccines
Two is the types of tests that were run
One stands for the day the pandemic's done.

Who knows the meaning of number nine?
If you know the answer, just give a sign.

Nine stands for the months of "Operation Warp Speed"
Producing the vaccines that we all need.

Eight stands for the work of the angels in white
Seven stands for the time we cheered each night
Six stands for the feet of social distance
Five stands for the financial assistance
Four streaming services on our screens
Three stands for the three approved vaccines
Two is the types of tests that were run
One stands for the day the pandemic's done.

Who knows the meaning of number ten?
Boys who know its meaning grow up good men.

Ten stands for the ten weekly Zoom meetings decreed
Where "Turn off your mute" we did frequently plead.
Nine stands for "Operation Warp Speed"
Eight stands for the work of the angels in white
Seven stands for the time we cheered each night
Six stands for the feet of social distance
Five stands for the financial assistance
Four streaming services on our screens
Three stands for the three approved vaccines
Two is the types of tests that were run
One stands for the day the pandemic's done.

Who knows the meaning of number eleven? If you want a hint, look up in heaven.

Eleven stands for the pounds added to our rear
From pandemic binging that gave us cheer

Ten stands for the ten Zoom meetings decreed
Nine stands for "Operation Warp Speed"
Eight stands for the work of the angels in white
Seven stands for the time we cheered each night
Six stands for the feet of social distance
Five stands for the financial assistance
Four streaming services on our screens
Three stands for the three approved vaccines
Two is the types of tests that were run
One stands for the day the pandemic's done.

Who knows the meaning of number twelve?
Into your knowledge of history delve.

Twelve stands for the months of boredom and fear
Before signs of hope began to appear
Eleven stands for the pounds added to our rear
Ten stands for the ten Zoom meetings decreed
Nine stands for "Operation Warp Speed"
Eight stands for the work of the angels in white
Seven stands for the time we cheered each night
Six stands for the feet of social distance
Five stands for the financial assistance
Four streaming services on our screens
Three stands for the three approved vaccines
Two is the types of tests that were run
One stands for the day the pandemic's done.

The leader raises the cup of wine and says:

We are about to drink the fourth cup of wine.
Let us all say together

LECHAYENU	לחיינו
MIKAMONU	מי כמונו
EIN ALEINU	אין עלינו

HERE'S TO US, WHO'S LIKE US? DAMN FEW.

Drink the fourth cup of wine.

Before we close, one final song, especially for the children. It tells the story of a man who got Covid, but because he had been vaccinated he didn't die, or even get very sick. (Unlike the poor goat in that other folk song, that got eaten by the cat that got bitten by the dog that, oh never mind). In fact, it wasn't much worse than a cold. But he still quarantined for two weeks and helped stop the spread.

A COVID BUG

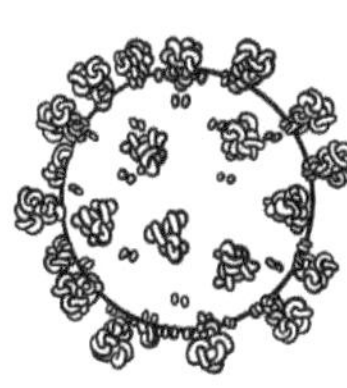

A Covid bug, a covid bug,
My father caught from two goyim
Covid bug, covid bug.

First came a mask
That stopped the bug
My father caught from two goyim
Covid bug, covid bug.

Then came a doctor
That wore a mask
That stopped the bug
My father caught from two goyim
Covid bug, covid bug.

Then came the science
That helped the doctor
That wore a mask
That stopped the bug
My father caught from two goyim
Covid bug, covid bug.

Then came the test
That proved the science
That helped the doctor
That wore a mask
That stopped the bug
My father caught from two goyim
Covid bug, covid bug.

Then came the drug
That passed the test
That proved the science
That helped the doctor
That wore a mask
That stopped the bug
My father caught from two goyim
Covid bug, covid bug.

Then came the shot
That held the drug
That passed the test
That proved the science
That helped the doctor
That wore a mask
That stopped the bug
My father caught from two goyim
Covid bug, covid bug.

Then came the nurse, praised be she
Who gave the shot
That held the drug
That passed the test
That proved the science
That helped the doctor
That wore a mask
That stopped the bug
My father caught from two goyim
Covid bug, covid bug.

THE CLOSE

Now we come to the end of our Un-Seder Service.

Once again we have mutilated the age-old epic of Israel's liberation from bondage.

As we have celebrated this festival tonight, so may we celebrate a real seder, all of us together, next year in joy, in peace, in health, and in freedom.

SACK FAMILY POT ROAST RECIPE
(Complete with my mother's typos and editorial notes)

THIS IS SPELLED OUT FOR A NON COOK! FIRST ON THE LIST SHOULD BE DIRECTIONS TO THE KITCHEN

PASSOVER POT ROAST

I usually make about 18 pound of first cut brisket - it serves about 27/8 people

Ingredients

brisket
lipton's onion soup mix (one package)
hunt's tomato sauce - maybe two or three large cans
hunts tomato paste - maybe two small cans
onions
heinz ketchup
carrots
dry sherry

cut off most of fat from the meat - leave some so it can bown.

cut up enough onions to cover the bottom of the dutch oven - with as much meat as I use--I usually cook it in two pots.

then brown various pieces of meat over a medium flame on top of onions--both onions and meat will brown. If you have many pieces of meat in one pot - turn it when side is browned so all sides and ends can brown.

THEN - dump in the lipton's soup (one package for each pot) tomato sauce, tomato paste, ketchup --I really think that is what make the difference in the taste -add sherry - maybe half cup or little more to each pot - that also helps

cover

turn every thirty (30) minutes - if there is more than one piece in the pot - re-arrange when you turn-put bottom on top middle on bottom etc.--do that each time you turn - cook it for 3 hours that makes 6 turns - don't - do it - put on a timer and take several half hour naps.

cut up and scrape enough carrots to feed as many people as you have invited - more carrots may be made later and added. Dump in the carrots for the last hour.

MAKE A DAY AHEAD - TASTES BETTER THE SECOND DAY WHEN IT HAS BEEN SITTING IN THE GARAVY FOR AWHILE - ALSO -IT'S EASIER TO CUT.

Hope I haven't left anything out!!
EAT!!!!!!! - freeze leftovers

ACKNOWLEDGEMENTS

While this book was written in lockdown isolation, I could never have upgraded it from a fun diversion into a publishable book without some help.

Laverne Berry, my friend, my lawyer, and my favorite companion for depressing Broadway plays.

Janet Stilson and Deborah Brozina, my posse, proofreaders, and support team. Thank you Janet for providing publishing guidance and indulging my devotion to the Oxford comma and thank you Deb for indulging my, well, everything.

Arlynn Greenbaum, who set me on the path to publishing with an introduction and a vote of confidence.

Alix and Jessica Friedman, who supplied the Hebrew translation for the Sondheim lyric I used in the "prayer" over the wine.

www.ingramcontent.com/pod-product-compliance
Ingram Content Group UK Ltd.
Pitfield, Milton Keynes, MK11 3LW, UK
UKHW021925190726
13853UKWH00002B/861